Slow Cooker Cookbook for Beginners UK

1000-Day Delicious and Stress-free Recipes with Pictures using European Measurements to Enjoy Classic Dishes and New Favorites.

Gratto Zapanta

© **Copyright 2022 Gratto Zapanta - All Rights Reserved.**

In no way is it legal to reproduce, duplicate, or transmit any part of this document by either electronic means or in printed format. Recording of this publication is strictly prohibited, and any storage of this material is not allowed unless with written permission from the publisher. All rights reserved.

The information provided herein is stated to be truthful and consistent, in that any liability, regarding inattention or otherwise, by any usage or abuse of any policies, processes, or directions contained within is the solitary and complete responsibility of the recipient reader. Under no circumstances will any legal liability or blame be held against the publisher for any reparation, damages, or monetary loss due to the information herein, either directly or indirectly.

Respective authors own all copyrights not held by the publisher.

Legal Notice:

This book is copyright protected. This is only for personal use. You cannot amend, distribute, sell, use, quote or paraphrase any part of the content within this book without the consent of the author or copyright owner. Legal action will be pursued if this is breached.

Disclaimer Notice:

Please note the information contained within this document is for educational and entertainment purposes only. Every attempt has been made to provide accurate, up-to-date and reliable, complete information. No warranties of any kind are expressed or implied. Readers acknowledge that the author is not engaging in the rendering of legal, financial, medical or professional advice.

By reading this document, the reader agrees that under no circumstances are we responsible for any losses, direct or indirect, which are incurred as a result of the use of information contained within this document, including, but not limited to, errors, omissions, or inaccuracies.

Table of Contents

Introduction 5

Chapter 1: Breakfast 17

Chapter 2: Chicken 23

Chapter 3: Beef 30

Chapter 4: Lamb 37

Chapter 5: Pork 43

Chapter 6: Vegetable 50

Chapter 7: Soups 57

Chapter 8: Desserts 64

Conclusion 71

Appendix recipe Index 72

INTRODUCTION

A slow cooker is an electric device that cooks food for a long time at a low temperature. Slow cookers are excellent for breaking down and tenderizing big chunks of meat like pot roasts or beef stews because of this low-and-slow technique. But they have other options as well. A home cook's preferred method for making soups, ribs, dips, beverages, and bread is the slow cooker.

In addition to its adaptability, a slow cooker has a lot of other advantages, such as the ability to uniformly prepare food without needing to use your hands. Home cooks can now conduct other household chores, run errands, or start their day at the office because of this. Additionally, slow cookers are simple to use and typically only need to be plugged in.

How Do You Use a Slow Cooker?

Utilizing a slow cooker is easy. Simply preheat your slow cooker to low or high, add the ingredients for your chosen dinner, and then cover it and let it simmer. You may either keep your dinner warm in the slow cooker or turn the slow cooker off to turn off the heating element if you don't want to eat it straight away. Now I'm done!

Some of the components for some recipes, such ground beef chilli or pork chops, must first be browned in a skillet before being added to the slow cooker. Preheating your slow cooker in these situations might be a good idea.

What Can You Cook in a Slow Cooker?

Really, practically anything can be cooked in a slow cooker. The hearty slow-cooked soups, stews, and major dishes that benefit from simmering for hours on end, such chilli, meatloaf, pulled pork sandwiches, and shredded chicken tacos, are perhaps the ones you are most familiar with. One-pot meals like casseroles that are prepared in a slow cooker make dinner prep easy as well.

Since they can be cooked for the main meal, baked potatoes and vegetable dishes are popular slow-cooker side dishes. If you've ever had a sweet potato that was very crisp or a carrot that was mushy, Our Test Kitchen suggests being cautious about how you chop your potatoes and vegetables. Each ingredient must be equally prepared according to the formula. Larger pieces could be undercooked while smaller ones might be overcooked. Also, try to prepare softer vegetables, such as peas, spinach, or zucchini later in the cooking process. They won't crumble or turn fully mushy as a result of this.

You might not be aware of a few surprising applications for your slow cooker. You can make meals for hands-free breakfast and brunch using the slow cooker, including hash browns, oatmeal, and even cinnamon rolls. With the aid of slow-cooker appetisers like fondue or cheese dip, a party may also be organised ahead of time. Instead, try making a slow-cooker spaghetti dish; just be careful not to overcook the noodles to prevent grit.

A slow cooker is not required to prepare savoury foods. These dessert recipes for the slow cooker can be used to make cakes, puddings, candy clusters, and other sweet treats. Even better, treat yourself to a sweet beverage made in the slow cooker, such hot cocoa or tea with a tropical flavour.

Understand Your Slow Cooker

There are typically two or three settings on slow cookers. Food will be cooked in six to ten hours when utilising the low setting. It takes four to six hours for food to cook on the high setting. If at all feasible, cook for the first hour on high in the slow cooker before switching to the setting that best suits your needs. Two hours on low are about equivalent to one hour on high. At 350 degrees F, an hour in the oven is comparable to 4 hours on high or 8 hours on low. Similar to how 4-6 hours on high and 8-16 hours on low translate into 3 hours in the oven.

The capacity of slow cookers ranges from 1 to 7 quarts. Larger slow cookers are ideal for huge chunks of meat and soups, while smaller ones work well for dips or sauces. If you're just going to cook for four or fewer people, a slow cooker in the 3.5–4 quart range is excellent. If you want leftovers or will be cooking for five or more people, a slower cooker with a capacity of 5-7 quarts is recommended.

Benefits of using a slow cooker

The ability to cook a meal while everyone is away at work or school and then have a hot meal waiting for them when it's time for dinner makes slow cookers an indispensable equipment for many busy households nowadays. Let's examine more closely the benefits of having a slow cooker in your kitchen.

1.Slow cookers permit hands-off cooking

Slow cookers allow you to place your ingredients and leave them to cook, which is a great feature as it allows you to focus on other tasks while your meal cooks, unlike most appliances that demand a close eye or some amount of care.

Put the ingredients in the pot, choose your favourite settings, and then let the slow cooker handle the rest. People who have demanding schedules and little time to spare for meal preparation may find this option to be extremely helpful.

2.Using a slow cooker enhances the flavor of recipes

Slow cookers are renowned for their capacity to bring out the authentic flavor of a recipe. It mixes the varied qualities of the employed components, resulting in a dish that explodes with flavors and aromas that are pure and devoid of additives.

A slow cooker also enables the perfect flavor distribution because the contents simmer at such low temperatures, giving you a mouth-watering meal.

3.Slow cookers are excellent for making the meat tender.

This is why many venison dishes are frequently prepared in a slow cooker: with one by your side, you can easily tenderize tough meats or inexpensive cuts, making them smooth and tasty after a lengthy cooking process.

Less lean beef, roast, or chuck steaks can be tenderized in a slow cooker without having to pay more for the pricier cuts.

4. Slow cookers are simple to use and understand

To use your slow cooker, you don't need to be an expert cook or electrical device user. All you have to do is place everything in the slow cooker, choose your favourite settings, and turn it on.

Slow cookers don't take much practise to use, so beginners may create masterpieces with them. You may thoroughly prepare yourself to prepare a delicacy with this practical cooking tool by reading the user instructions. A slow cooker cookbook is highly beneficial for beginners.

5. Slow cookers encourage nutritious cooking

High heat is renowned for destroying nutrients in food, lowering the overall nutritional value of a cuisine. High temperatures can cause the release of potentially hazardous chemicals that can result in diabetes and kidney problems.

Slow cooking preserves nutrients while minimizing the generation of potentially dangerous compounds thanks to the extra-low temperatures used. Additionally, the likelihood of overcooking is much decreased when using a slow cooker because, unlike boiling or frying, you won't be cooking at high temperatures.

6. Do Slow Cookers Use Less Energy?

Slow cookers consume less energy than a typical electric oven, enabling you to make longer-term financial savings. Even though it is impractical to use a slow cooker for every meal, you can still save money by using it instead of other kitchen appliances.

You can save money on energy costs by preparing meals in bulk with a slow cooker rather than cooking them individually. Food prepared in slow cookers is typically consumed in multiple servings, which saves you money on ingredients.

7. Slow Cooker Clean-up Is Simple

Food is less likely to adhere to the bottom of the pan while cooking at low temperatures as opposed to when using an electric oven. You'll appreciate the fact that cooking meals in a crockpot mean washing fewer dishes afterward.

8. Various Types of Slow Cookers

Slow cookers are now more adaptable than ever thanks to technological improvements, and some even have programmable settings. Basic slow cookers often include manual on/off switches and settings for hot, medium, keep warm, or low temperatures.

The availability of a wide range of settings and the inclusion of electronic timing devices in modern slow cookers enable the cooker to undertake numerous tasks when making meals.

9. You can serve food without having to reheat it in slow cookers.

Typically, it takes longer for food from a slow cooker to chill fully. Even better, the majority of contemporary slow cookers have "keep warm settings" that let your food stay warm after cooking is finished.

10. The Best Time Saver: Slow Cookers

Food can be prepared in a slow cooker while you are occupied with other tasks. Because it doesn't need much focus, it's ideal for situations where you're too weary or simply want to avoid adding another task to your list.

There is no need for constant supervision or checking every few minutes when all the components are placed within this gadget and turned on. In fact, many recipes suggest never opening the lid while cooking!

This means that you can spend some quality time doing anything else while your food cooks away within its tiny pot-shaped housing, such as catching up on household duties or even taking a quick nap until dinner time again.

The Ideal Meat for Your Slow Cooker

Although practically any type of meat can be cooked in a slow cooker, we recommend avoiding dry meat by choosing portions that are tougher or have more fat because they withstand prolonged cooking better. So, pig shoulder is chosen over tenderloin, beef chuck roast is preferred over strip steak, and chicken thighs are preferred over chicken breasts. If you want to prepare lean meat, you might need to shorten the cooking time. A thermometer can accurately determine when the meat is done.

Only few types of meat can be prepared in a slow cooker from frozen. You can find the dos and don't on this list.

Beef: With a little assistance from your skillet, our slow cooker beef recipes, including briskets and ground beef dishes, come together quickly.

Chicken: Slow cooker chicken recipes are some of our playbook's simplest recipes. From tender slow-cooked chicken breasts to slow-cooked roast chicken, we can demonstrate how to make it all.

Pork: Using a slow cooker to prepare pulled pork, country ribs, and ham is one of our favourites. After one mouthful, you'll be a lover of these slow cooker pork recipes.

Sausage: Use these delectable slow cooker sausage recipes to put your Italian and kielbasa sausage to use.

Turkey: Thanksgiving dinners will be stress-free thanks to these slow-cooker turkey breast recipes, while any night of the year will be wonderful for these slow-cooker ground turkey dishes.

Slow Cooker Safety and Tips

If you are hesitant to leave your slow cooker on while you are gone all day, think about preparing meals at different times when you are home, even while you are asleep. Once the food has completed cooking, cool it down and store it in the refrigerator before reheating it on the stovetop or in the oven for a later dinner.

Here are some fundamental safety guidelines and pointers for using a slow cooker:

1. Before using your slow cooker, grease the interior of the stoneware or spray it with non-stick cooking spray for simple clean-up and maintenance. Liners for slow cookers make clean-up simpler.
2. Prior to cooking frozen meat and poultry in a slow cooker, always thaw them in the refrigerator. Do not use frozen meat in your slow cooker to ensure proper cooking.
3. No less than half and no more than two-thirds of the slow cooker should be filled. A slow cooker's capacity can have an impact on cooking time, food quality, and safety.
4. Vegetables should go in the slow cooker first because they cook more slowly than meat and poultry. Top the vegetables with the meat and a liquid, such as broth, water, or sauce.
5. Add the liquid called for in the recipe, such as broth, water, or barbecue sauce. When adopting a non-slow cooker recipe for use in a slow cooker, you can typically reduce liquids by one-third to one-half because liquids do not boil away in a slow cooker.
6. If at all possible, start cooking in your slow cooker on high for the first hour, then reduce the heat to low to finish.
7. When cooking, keep the cover on. Cooking time is slowed by removing the cover. Approximately 15 to 20 minutes of cooking time are wasted each time the lid is raised.
8. Pasta or other grains should be added at the end of cooking to avoid becoming mushy. Pasta or another grain, such as rice, may need to be cooked separately and added right before serving.
9. To avoid curdling, add milk, cheese, and cream during the final hour.
10. Tomatoes, mushrooms, and zucchini are examples of very soft vegetables that can be added during the final 45 minutes of cooking.

Various Designs for Slow Cookers

There is a vast variety of slow cookers available on the market right now. Although they all function in the same way technically, the features and construction quality might differ greatly.

You can get a slow cooker with three heat settings: keep warm, low, and hot, depending on the model. Some slow cookers, however, feature a fourth heat setting called medium, which is rarely used in recipes.

Slow cookers can vary greatly from brand to brand, and each has its own unique advantages and disadvantages. Some people use ceramic pots, while others use metal ones. While some utilize metal or ceramic lids, others use glass. The majority of these variations are negligible and mostly merely a matter of taste.

A lot of contemporary slow cookers come with a tonne of functionality. For instance, practically all devices now feature programmable timers, which are quite useful if you are not at home the entire day to monitor the food's preparation.

Additionally, there are slow cookers with built-in Wi-Fi, more heat settings, and many other features. Most of these features aren't strictly necessary, but depending on your situation, they might be useful.

To make sure you are purchasing a slow cooker that can accomplish what it is intended to do correctly, I advise reading product reviews. A crock pot is a well-known brand of slow cooker that typically ensures a certain degree of quality and features.

Cleaning a Slow Cooker

Even while you might be tempted to use abrasive cleaners to remove stubborn stains, all you really need to clean a slow cooker with are a few common home items that you probably already have.

Baking soda is a mild abrasive that also brightens surfaces and acts as a natural deodorizer to get rid of aromas from foods like onions, garlic, and other stains. White vinegar that has been distilled is another useful natural cleaning agent. Together, these low-cost components produce a potent clean that won't damage your kitchen appliance's cooking surface or hardware.

Step 1, unplug the appliance, then add the cleaning agent.

Cut the slow cooker's power. Warm water should be added to the slow cooker. Slowly add half a cup of distilled white vinegar to the slow cooker. The amount of vinegar can be increased to 1 cup for slow cookers larger than 3 quarts.

Step 2 : Add baking soda in

Slowly add 1/2 cup baking soda to the slow cooker, waiting for any bubbles to go away before adding more. For a larger slow cooker, you can raise this amount by up to 1 cup.

Step 3 : Run on Low in

Put the slow cooker's lid on. Low-temperature setting; leave running for one hour. Before carrying out the subsequent instructions, switch off the slow cooker and remove the solution before letting the appliance to cool down.

Step 4 : Clean the slow cooker in

Cleaning your slow cooker shouldn't take too much effort since the heat will combine with the baking soda and vinegar to perform the heavy lifting for you. To remove any last bits of food, clean the area with a toothbrush or sponge.

Step 5: Clean Up

Clean the interior and exterior of the slow cooker with a cloth after rinsing it with water.

Frequently Asked Questions

What purpose does a slow cooker serve?

Because they cook food for an extended period of time at a moderate temperature, slow cookers help to tenderise less expensive cuts of meat. Slow cooking enhances the flavour of food. Casseroles, soups, stews, and one-pot dinners are just a few of the numerous foods that may be made in a slow cooker. In comparison to ovens, slow cookers consume less electricity..

How does a slow cooker function? What is it?

A slow cooker is a kitchen appliance that uses electricity to cook food slowly and at a low temperature. Because of this low-and-slow method, slow cookers are great for breaking down and tenderising large portions of meat like pot roasts or beef stews.

What meal types cannot be prepared in a slow cooker?

There are eleven things you shouldn't put in a slow cooker.

- leaner cuts of meat.

- Uncooked meat
- The fluid level is excessive.
- ... tender veggies.
- The temperature is too high.
- Dairy. ...
- Alcohol in excess.
- meat that still has its skin on.
- Rice and pasta
- Seafood
- Fresh, tender herbs

What are some common errors that people who use slow cookers make?

- Allow this gadget to do its job of making your life simpler.
- An excessive addition of liquid.
- Not Defrosting First.
- Overheating when cooking meat
- Improperly processing flavors-rich ingredients.
- Vegetable addition: It's too soon.
- Fully packing the slow cooker.
- taking off the pot's lid while the food is cooking.
- using a tender beef cut.

Is a slow cooker suitable for novices?

For a novice cook, a college student, or a busy parent who doesn't want a lot of fuss, the slow cooker is a terrific tool.

Why don't vegetables cook in slow cookers?

Adding frozen meat or veggies could prolong the time it takes for the slow cooker to reach temperature because it operates at a very low heat. Because it takes so long for the food to reach a safe temperature, this lengthens the cooking process and raises the risk of food poisoning.

What are the slow cooker's two key advantages?

They may be used all year round and consume less electricity than an oven. Slow cookers aid in the tenderization of less expensive meat cuts because of the prolonged, low-temperature cooking. As long as all the ingredients are in the slow cooker, preparation normally just requires one step, saving time and requiring less cleaning.

What happens if you cook meat slowly without browning it first?

Before putting ground beef in a slow cooker, it should always be browned and drained. If not, it could clump and leave the dish greasier.

Chapter 1: Breakfast

Slow Cooker Bread Recipe

Prep Time: 15 Minutes
Cook Time: 2 Hours   Serves: 10

Ingredients:

- 400g strong white bread flour
- 7g dried active yeast
- 2 tsp salt
- 1 tbsp sugar (optional)
- 250ml warm water
- 2 tbsp olive oil

Directions:

1. Switch slow cooker to high
2. Mix the flour, yeast, salt and sugar (if you are using) in a bowl.
3. Make a well in the middle and slowly add the water and oil, stirring it in as you do.
4. Get your hands in to combine the dough into a ball - to stop the dough sticking to your hands, rub a little oil on them.
5. Sprinkle flour on a work top counter and knead the dough for about 5 to 10 minutes.
6. Line the slow cooker with some greaseproof paper and place the dough on top.
7. Put the slow cooker lid on top and cook for 2 hours, check on it at the 90 minute mark to see if it is ready (some slow cookers cook faster than others).
8. If you prefer a firmer crust, put it under a grill for 5 minutes.
9. Leave the bread to rest for 10 minutes before slicing.

Nutritional Value (Amount per Serving):

Calories: 174; Fat: 3.42; Carb: 30.1; Protein: 5.08

Slow Cooker Bread

Prep Time: 15 Minutes
Cook Time: 2 Hours   Serves: 10

Ingredients:

- 400g strong white bread flour
- 7g dried active yeast
- 2 tsp salt
- 1 tbsp sugar (optional)
- 250ml warm water
- 2 tbsp olive oil

Directions:

1. Switch slow cooker to high
2. Mix the flour, yeast, salt and sugar (if you are using) in a bowl.
3. Make a well in the middle and slowly add the water and oil, stirring it in as you do.
4. Get your hands in to combine the dough into a ball - to stop the dough sticking to your hands, rub a little oil on them.
5. Sprinkle flour on a work top counter and knead the dough for about 5 to 10 minutes.
6. Line the slow cooker with some greaseproof paper and place the dough on top.
7. Put the slow cooker lid on top and cook for 2 hours, check on it at the 90 minute mark to see if it is ready (some slow cookers cook faster than others).
8. If you prefer a firmer crust, put it under a grill for 5 minutes.
9. Leave the bread to rest for 10 minutes before slicing.

Nutritional Value (Amount per Serving):

Calories: 174; Fat: 3.42; Carb: 30.1; Protein: 5.08

Carrot Cake Porridge

Prep Time: 10 Minutes
Cook Time: 8 Hours   Serves: 4

Ingredients:

- 150g Co-op porridge oats
- 1 litre unsweetened almond drink
- 1 carrot, finely grated
- 1 apple, grated
- 2 tsp ground cinnamon
- 50g Co-op sultanas
- ½ tsp ground ginger
- o Serve:
- 1 apple, thinly sliced
- 2 tbsp Co-op seed mix
- 1 tbsp Co-op sultanas

Directions:

1. Put all the ingredients for the porridge into your slow cooker
2. Stir well to combine, then cook on low for 8 hours
3. In the morning, if a skin has formed, simply stir it through the porridge
4. Serve in bowls sprinkled with the toppings

Nutritional Value (Amount per Serving):

Calories: 159; Fat: 3.12; Carb: 41.63; Protein: 7.29

Slow Cooker Stuffing Recipe

Prep Time: 20 Minutes
Cook Time: 4 Hours   Serves: 6

Ingredients:

- 196 g bread cubes about 1 loaf of bread
- 151.5 g celery chopped
- 120 g onions chopped
- 3.7 g sage
- 2.46 g salt
- 5.96 floz chicken broth
- 141.88 g butter melted

Directions:

1. Combine all ingredients minus the butter until well mixed

2. Toss with butter
3. Cook on low for 4-5 hours

Nutritional Value (Amount per Serving):

Calories: 270; Fat: 20.44; Carb: 18.86; Protein: 3.59

Slow Cooker Cherry Oatmeal

Prep Time: 10 Minutes
Cook Time: 8 Hours   Serves: 8

Ingredients:

- 240 g long cooking oats
- 90 g powdered sugar
- 595.34 g cherry pie filling
- 50.73 floz water
- 1/4 tsp salt

Directions:

1. Combine oats, sugar, salt, in a sprayed crock pot.
2. Add in cherry pie filling and water
3. Cook on low for 8 hours

Nutritional Value (Amount per Serving):

Calories: 203; Fat: 2.16; Carb: 51.93; Protein: 5.47

Slow Cooker Banana Oatmeal

Prep Time: 10 Minutes
Cook Time: 4 Hours   Serves: 6

Ingredients:

- 160 g steel cut oats
- 2-3 bananas ripe or overripe
- 1 c water
- 1 c heavy whipping cream
- 2 c whole milk
- 110 g brown sugar
- 1 tsp vanilla
- dash salt

Directions:

1. Line a slow cooker with parchment paper

2. Place the steel cut oats in the slow cooker bowl
3. Mix the liquids together in a separate bowl and add to the oats
4. Mash the bananas in a separate bowl until smooth and add to the oat mixture
5. Cook on low for 4 – 5 hours, or on high for 2 – 3, depending on the texture you prefer (longer for softer oats).

Nutritional Value (Amount per Serving):

Calories: 312; Fat: 14.36; Carb: 49.19; Protein: 8.31

Slow Cooker French Toast

Prep Time: 20 Minutes
Cook Time: 3 Hours   Serves: 6-8

Ingredients:

- Butter, for greasing
- 1 large brioche, preferably day-old
- 8 large eggs
- 475 ml single cream
- 70 g caster sugar
- 1 tsp. vanilla extract
- 1/2 tsp. ground cinnamon
- 1/4 tsp. salt
- small pinch nutmeg
- Maple syrup, for serving
- Icing sugar, for serving

Directions:

1. Lightly grease the inside of slow cooker with butter. Slice brioche into thick slices then quarter each slice. Place bread in slow cooker.
2. In a large bowl, combine eggs, single cream, sugar, ½ teaspoon cinnamon, vanilla, salt and nutmeg and beat until well combined. Pour egg mixture over bread, folding bread gently to make sure each piece is coated.
3. Cook on low for 2 ½ to 3 hours, until the French toast is warm and cooked through.
4. Serve warm with maple syrup and icing sugar.

Nutritional Value (Amount per Serving):

Calories: 290; Fat: 20.52; Carb: 22.22; Protein: 4.99

Chapter 2: Chicken

Slow Cooker Sweet And Sour Chicken

Prep Time: 10 Minutes
Cook Time: 5 Hours   Serves: 4

Ingredients:

- 8 boneless chicken thighs
- 1 clove garlic, crushed
- 1 onion, chopped
- 1 red pepper, deseeded and sliced
- 1 green pepper, deseeded and sliced
- 2 carrots, chopped
- weet And Sour Sauce
- 1 can (250ml) pineapple pieces
- 3 tbsp tomato ketchup
- 2 tbsp cornflour
- 150ml apple cider vinegar
- 100g brown sugar
- 1 tbsp soy sauce

Directions:

1. Prepare the sweet and sour sauce by mixing all the ingredients together. If you prefer a less tangy taste to your sweet and sour, reduce the amount of cider vinegar to 100ml.
2. Add the chicken pieces to the slow cooker and add the garlic, onions and carrots. You can optionally add the peppers now or add them 30 minutes before the end of the cooking time, depending on how well done you want them to be.
3. Pour the sweet and sour sauce over the top and place the lid on.
4. Set off on low for 5 to 6 hours, or high for 4 hours.

Nutritional Value (Amount per Serving):

Calories: 1162; Fat: 60.93; Carb: 103.53; Protein: 52.37

Slow Cooker Chicken And Prawn Paella Recipe

Prep Time: 10 Minutes
Cook Time: 2 Hours 30 Minutes
  Serves: 3

Ingredients:

- 1tbspolive oil
- 1chopped onion
- 1tspsmoked paprika
- 1tspthyme
- 300grisotto or paella rice
- 400gtin of chopped tomatoes
- 700mlchicken stock
- 350gfrozen cooked prawns

Directions:

1. Lightly fry the chopped onion in olive oil.
2. Add the paprika & thyme.
3. Measure out the rice and add this to the frying pan.
4. Fry for 1-2 minutes, stirring frequently. Place into the slow cooker pot.
5. Add your stock cubes. Or fresh stock if you're fancy.
6. Add the water for the stock.
7. Add the tinned tomatoes. Stir and then leave to cook on high for 2 hours.
8. Add the frozen prawns or other seafood. Cook for a further 30 minutes or until the seafood is cooked through and the rice has softened.
9. Serve! I often chopped chorizo at the last minute and it is delicious.

Nutritional Value (Amount per Serving):

Calories: 539; Fat: 12.37; Carb: 58.35; Protein: 50.48

Slow Cooker Chicken Tikka Masala

Prep Time: 5 Minutes
Cook Time: 4 Hours   Serves: 2

Ingredients:

- 1red onion
- 15mlolive oil
- 1tablespoonof Tikka Masala Mix
- 2clovesof garlic
- Salt + pepper

- 300gchicken thighboneless
- 30gtomato puree/tomato paste
- 200mlchicken stock
- 100gsoured cream

Directions:

1. Add the olive oil to your pot or pan. Finely chop your red onion. Lightly fry this, until translucent. This usually takes me around 3-4 minutes.
2. Add Tikka Masala spice mix and stir until well coated.
3. Crush or grate the garlic. Cook for 1 minute.
4. Add your chicken thigh. Stir to ensure everything is mixed evenly. You want to cook the chicken until it is lightly browned on the outside, but it doesn't need to be cooked through.
5. Season well with salt & pepper.
6. Add the tomato puree and stir, cook for 1 minute.
7. Add the chicken stock.
8. Cook on high for 4+ hours or low for 8+ hours.
9. 15 minutes before serving stir through the soured cream and mix well.
10. Once sufficiently warmed back through serve with add a little coriander to the top.
11. Serve alongside your favourite rice (we make slow cooker rice sometimes) and with a nice naan bread, or other suitable accompaniments. We love Bombay potatoes or onion bhajis!

Nutritional Value (Amount per Serving):

Calories: 777; Fat: 49.2; Carb: 32.59; Protein: 51.01

Slow Cooker Chicken Mushroom Pie Filling Recipe

Prep Time: 5 Minutes
Cook Time: 10 Hours   Serves: 2

Ingredients:

- 250 ml white wine
- 2 tbsp of plain flour
- salt and pepper
- stock cube or stock pot
- 1 tin of sliced mushrooms or 300g fresh mushrooms
- 400 g chicken breast
- 1 tsp thyme or tarragon or rosemary
- 20 g butter
- 50 g frozen filo pastry sheets (approximate weight)

Directions:

1. Slow cooker chicken mushroom pie filling
2. Whisk together 250ml of white wine, 2 tablespoons of plain flour and salt + pepper. Either whisk it in a jug, to measure the wine, or directly in your slow cooker pot to save effort.
3. Add your chicken and the mushrooms.
4. Crumble in a stock cube or add a stock pot.
5. Add a little thyme, tarragon or rosemary depending on your preferred flavour.
6. Cook on low for 8+ hours. If you want to keep larger chunks of chicken then used diced chicken and cook for 4-5 hours on low or 3 hours on high.
7. Filo pie topping
8. Pour your filling into a pie tin.
9. Melt your butter.
10. Dip your filo pastry sheets in and then lay on top of the slow cooker chicken mushroom pie filling.
11. Cook 190°C for 25-30 minutes. As soon as the top is golden brown it is ready for serving.

Nutritional Value (Amount per Serving):

Calories: 963; Fat: 48.76; Carb: 16.34; Protein: 112.99

Slow Cooker Cream Cheese Chicken

Prep Time: 5 Minutes
Cook Time: 9 Hours   Serves: 4

Ingredients:

- 5 boneless, skinless chicken breasts
- 2 tbsp Italian seasoning
- 1/2 tsp celery seed
- 1 tbsp onion powder
- 1/4 tsp pepper
- 1 tsp salt
- 2 garlic cloves, minced
- 2 284ml cans Cream of Mushroom soup
- 1 250g package cream cheese, softened, cut into cubes
- 1 tbsp chives, chopped

Directions:

1. Place chicken breasts in the slow cooker.
2. In a small bowl, stir together Italian seasoning, celery seed, onion powder, pepper, salt and garlic cloves. Sprinkle on top of chicken.

3. Pour the cans of mushroom soup on top of chicken.
4. Cook on LOW for 8 hours.
5. Shred the chicken with two forks. Add the cream cheese and cook on HIGH for 1 hour.
6. Stir the melted cream cheese to mix everything together. Sprinkle chives on top. Serve hot.

Nutritional Value (Amount per Serving):

Calories: 1378; Fat: 59; Carb: 144.71; Protein: 64.74

Slow Cooker Teriyaki Chicken

Prep Time: 10 Minutes
Cook Time: 4 Hours   Serves: 4

Ingredients:

- 60ml low sodium soy sauce
- 60ml water
- 110g honey
- 3 tablespoons mirin or rice vinegar
- 2 teaspoons toasted sesame oil
- 3 cloves garlic minced
- 2 teaspoons fresh ginger grated
- 700g chicken breasts boneless skinless
- 2 tablespoons cornstarch
- 1 teaspoon toasted sesame seeds
- 2 tablespoons green onions sliced

Directions:

1. In a small bowl or jug, combine soy sauce, water, honey, vinegar, sesame oil, garlic, and ginger, and give it a whisk.
2. Place the chicken in the slow cooker. Pour the sauce you just made in the small bowl over the chicken.
3. Cover the slow cooker with the lid and cook on high for 2-2.5 hours or on low for 6 hours.
4. The chicken is ready when the internal temperature of the thickest part of the breast reaches 74°C with an instant-read thermometer.
5. Take the chicken out of the crockpot and shred it.
6. Remove the sauce from the slow cooker, strain it, and add it to a small saucepan.
7. Mix 2 tablespoons of cornstarch with 1 tablespoon of water. Whisk together.
8. On medium high heat, heat the sauce. Then, add in a cornstarch slurry. Bring the mixture to a boil, and whisk until the sauce thickens.

9. Toss the shredded chicken in the sauce.
10. Serve the extra saucy chicken with cooked jasmine rice, quinoa, brown rice, or fried rice and garnish with toasted sesame seeds and sliced green onions.

Nutritional Value (Amount per Serving):

Calories: 348; Fat: 7.24; Carb: 28.52; Protein: 41.13

Slow-Cooker Sweet And Sour Chicken

Prep Time: 10 Minutes
Cook Time: 1 Hour   Serves: 4

Ingredients:

- 1-2 tbsp olive oil
- 500g skinless chicken thigh fillets, diced
- 1 red onion, diced
- 1 red pepper, sliced
- 1 green pepper, sliced
- 3 cloves garlic, crushed
- a thumb-sized piece ginger, finely grated
- 1 red chill, deseeded and finely chopped
- 400ml chicken stock, just-boiled if cooking on the hob (or 200ml if using the slow cooker)
- 30g soft light brown sugar
- 4 tbsp tomato ketchup
- 2 tbsp apple cider vinegar
- 1 tsp cornflour
- 1 tbsp soy sauce
- 1 spring onion, sliced (optional)

Directions:

1. Heat the oil in a heavy-based casserole over a medium heat. Cook the chicken for 4 minutes or until golden.
2. Add the onion, peppers, garlic, ginger and chilli, and cook for 1-2 minutes. Add the stock, sugar, ketchup and vinegar, then give it a good stir. Put a lid on, reduce the heat to low and cook for 45 minutes
3. Whisk together the cornflour and 1 tbsp of water in a small bowl, then add to the pan, stirring until thickened. Just before serving, add the soy sauce to taste, then sprinkle over the spring onions, if using.

Nutritional Value (Amount per Serving):

Calories: 686; Fat: 40.29; Carb: 21.55; Protein: 57.57

Chapter 3: Beef

Slow-Cooker Spiced Beef Brisket With Cranberries

Prep Time: 30 Minutes
Cook Time: 8 Hours   Serves: 10

Ingredients:

- 2 tbsp pomegranate molasses (or 1 tbsp each honey and balsamic vinegar)
- zest of 2 clementines
- 1 tbsp chopped thyme leaves
- ¼ tsp ground allspice
- ½ tsp paprika
- 1 tsp ground cinnamon
- 1.7kg beef brisket
- 2 tbsp olive oil
- 2 red onions, finely sliced
- 3 celery sticks, finely diced
- 300ml hot beef stock - use gluten-free stock if required
- 1 star anise
- 1 cinnamon stick
- 300g fresh or frozen cranberries
- 5 garlic cloves, finely chopped
- 1 tbsp red wine vinegar
- 75g dark brown muscovado sugar
- ½ x 30g pack flat-leaf parsley

Directions:

1. In a large bowl, mix together the pomegranate molasses, clementine zest, thyme, and ground spices. Season with black pepper only, no salt. Unwrap the beef, keeping it rolled, and pat dry with kitchen paper. Transfer to the bowl and turn in the marinade to coat. Cover and set aside in the fridge for at least an hour or up to a day ahead, to marinate. Remove from the fridge an hour before cooking.
2. When ready to cook, heat half the oil in a large frying pan. Add the red onions, celery and garlic and cook gently over a low heat for 10 minutes. Stir in the red wine vinegar, then transfer to the slow cooker, cover with the lid and put on the low setting. Return the pan to a high heat with the remaining tablespoon of oil, and when hot add the beef, leaving any residual marinade behind. Sear on all sides to brown, then transfer to the slow cooker along with the hot stock, remaining marinade, star anise and cinnamon stick. Replace the lid and continue to cook on the low setting for 6 hours.
3. After 6 hours, turn over the beef; add the cranberries and sugar. Replace the lid; cook for 2 hours until the beef is fall-apart tender.
4. After the full 8 hours, lift out the beef, transfer to a plate and cover with foil to keep warm. Strain the stock and cranberry mixture (reserving the fruits),

and bring to the boil. Bubble for about 15 minutes or until reduced to about 350ml. Season to taste, or sweeten slightly, if needed.
5. Cut away any string from the beef and discard, then shred the meat with two forks. Toss with the reduced sauce and the reserved fruit mixture, discarding the whole spices.
6. Pile on to a platter; chop the parsley and scatter over the beef.

Nutritional Value (Amount per Serving):

Calories: 362; Fat: 11.98; Carb: 27.05; Protein: 37.24

Slow Cooker Chinese Beef Broccoli

Prep Time: 5 Minutes
Cook Time: 4 Hours   Serves: 4

Ingredients:

- 1 tbsp groundnut oil (or similar)
- 2 onions, thinly sliced
- 4 cloves garlic, crushed and chopped
- 600g stewing steak
- 250ml beef stock
- 60 ml soy sauce
- 3 tbsp oyster sauce
- 1 tbsp brown sugar
- 1 tsp Chinese 5-spice
- 1 head broccoli, cut into small florets
- 4 shiitake mushrooms, halved (optional)
- 1 tbsp Chinese rice wine (optional)

Directions:

1. Optional first step: select the SAUTE program, select BEEF STEAK and press START. Add oil and allow to heat. Add the beef in batches and stir regularly for ~3 minutes until browned. Then add the onion and soften for a further 3 minutes. Press the BACK button.
2. Select the SLOW COOK function and scroll down to BEEF STEW. Adjust the cooking time to 4 hours, add all the rest of the ingredients apart from the broccoli and press START (see note above about the broccoli).
3. When the cooking program has finished, assuming you did not add the broccoli in step 2 then add the broccoli, press the BACK button and select the SAUTE function, select BEEF STEAK and press START. This will boil the broccoli for 7 minutes and it should be nicely cooked with a little bit of crunch.

Nutritional Value (Amount per Serving):

Calories: 221; Fat: 8.1; Carb: 25.18; Protein: 13.53

Winter Slow Cooker Beef Braise With Redcurrant Port Sauce

Prep Time: 10 Minutes
Cook Time: 20 Minutes   Serves: 4

Ingredients:

- raised Chuck Steak
- 750g of chuck steak, trimmed of excess fat and cut into 5cm chunks
- 2 large onions, peeled and diced
- 2 garlic cloves, peeled and finely diced
- 4 tbsp of ruby port, or tawny port
- 6 tbsp of redcurrant jelly
- 150ml of beef stock
- salt
- pepper
- umplings
- 225g of self-raising flour
- 110g of shredded vegetable suet, or grated frozen butter
- salt
- pepper
- o Serve
- redcurrant jelly
- mixed vegetables, steamed
- mashed potatoes, or champ

Directions:

1. Turn your slow cooker on to the high setting.
2. Place all of the ingredients, except the dumpling mixture, into the slow cooker and cook for 6–8 hours.
3. 1 hour before the end of the cooking time, make the dumplings by mixing the suet into the flour. Season and mix to a soft dough with gradual additions of water
4. Shape the dumplings into 6–8 balls, drop on top of the casserole in the slow cooker, replace the lid and cook for a further hour until it is ready to serve.
5. Serve immediately with your choice of seasonal greens and some mashed potato or champ

Nutritional Value (Amount per Serving):

Calories: 1032; Fat: 52.17; Carb: 87.08; Protein: 56.26

Slow Cooker Crock Pot Tater Tot Casserole Recipe

Prep Time: 20 Minutes
Cook Time: 3 Hours   Serves: 8

Ingredients:

- 0.45 kg ground beef browned
- 1 Rotel
- 481.94 g Tater Tots frozen
- 1 Cream of Chicken Soup
- 1 onion small
- 226 g cheddar cheese shredded

Directions:

1. Brown beef and add in chopped onion and Rotel
2. Pour beef and onion mixture on the bottom of a greased Crock Pot
3. Mix in Cream of Chicken Soup
4. Top with tater tots across the top
5. Cook low for 2-3 hours.
6. 30 minutes before you are going to serve the Tater Tot Casserole top with shredded cheese.

Nutritional Value (Amount per Serving):

Calories: 295; Fat: 14.74; Carb: 19.67; Protein: 20.47

Guinness Corned Beef And Cabbage

Prep Time: 10 Minutes
Cook Time: 8 Hours   Serves: 10

Ingredients:

- 10 Baby red potatoes quartered
- 1 Onion peeled cut into pieces
- 1 l Water
- 1.81 kg Corned beef brisket with spice packet
- 6 ounces Guinness
- 0.5 Cabbage coarsely chopped

Directions:

1. Place onions and potatoes in the bottom of the Crock-Pot
2. Pour in water and place brisket on top

3. Pour beer over brisket, It is about a half a can so enjoy the 2nd half as you cook
4. Sprinkle brisket with spices set Crock Pot on high
5. Cook 8 hours on high, 1 hour before serving stir in cabbage pieces and recover crock pot

Nutritional Value (Amount per Serving):

Calories: 629; Fat: 27.52; Carb: 61.75; Protein: 33.87

Slow Cooker Brisket With Golden Ale Gravy Horseradish Mash

Prep Time: 30 minutes
Cook Time: 8 Hrs And 30 Minutes
Serves: 6

Ingredients:

- 1.2kg brisket, rolled
- 2 tbsp vegetable oil, plus extra for drizzling
- 2 large onions, sliced
- 4 tbsp plain flour
- 500-550ml golden ale
- 1 tbsp yeast or beef extract
- 1 tbsp dark brown soft sugar, plus extra to taste
- 1 tbsp balsamic vinegar, plus extra to taste
- ½ bunch of thyme
- 2 bay leaves
- 500ml hot beef stock
- 2 tsp cornflour (optional)
- or The Horseradish Mash
- 2kg Maris Piper or other floury potatoes, chopped
- 4 tbsp horseradish
- 100g butter
- 100g crème fraîche
- handful of parsley, chopped

Directions:

1. Season the brisket all over with salt and pepper. Heat the vegetable oil in a frying pan (or use the sear function on your slow cooker) and sear the meat all over until browned. Transfer to a plate. Add another drizzle of oil, if needed, and fry the onions with a pinch of salt until lightly golden, about

12 minutes. Sprinkle over the flour, stir until well-mixed, then pour in the ale and scrape the bottom of the pan to pick up any browned bits. Tip everything into the slow cooker (if using a frying pan).

2. Add the yeast or beef extract, sugar and vinegar, then the beef and herbs. Top up with stock until the brisket is just over half submerged. Cover and cook for 7-8 hrs on low until tender. Remove the meat from the slow cooker and cover to keep warm. Use the reduce or simmer function on your slow cooker and simmer for 10-15 minutes until the gravy has thickened to your liking. If your slow cooker doesn't have a simmer function, pour the gravy into a pan and simmer on the hob until thickened. Add a pinch more salt, sugar or a dash more vinegar if needed. If you like your gravy to be extra-thick, mix the cornflour with a splash of cold water, then add to the pan and bubble for a few minutes.

3. Just before you remove the meat from the slow cooker, start on the mash. Cook the potatoes in a pan of boiling salted water for 20 minutes until very tender when pressed. Drain and steam-dry for a few minutes before mashing with the horseradish, butter and crème fraîche. Scatter with parsley to serve. Cut the brisket into wedges and serve with the gravy and mash.

Nutritional Value (Amount per Serving):

Calories: 1439; Fat: 42.62; Carb: 191.05; Protein: 75.07

Chapter 4: Lamb

Slow Cooker Lamb Osso Bucco

Prep Time: 15 Minutes
Cook Time: 4-8 Hours   Serves: 4-6

Ingredients:

- 800g lamb shoulder or leg meat cut into 2 inch pieces
- Flour for dusting
- 4 tbsp olive oil
- 2 carrots diced
- 2 stalks celery diced
- 2 medium onions chopped
- 2 cloves garlic chopped
- 1tsp fresh thyme, chopped
- 1 tin chopped tomatoes
- 250ml white wine
- 200ml beef stock
- or The Gremolata
- 15g chopped flat leaf parsley
- zest of 1 lemon, plus extra to decorate
- 1 garlic clove, finely chopped

Directions:

1. Turn the slow cooker on. Season and dust the lamb pieces with flour. Heat 1 tbsp oil in a large frying pan. Sear the meat on all sides and then remove and place in the slow cooker.
2. Heat the remaining olive oil and add the carrots, onions, celery, garlic, thyme and some salt and pepper. Sauté for 10 minutes and then add the wine, stock and tomatoes. Bring to a boil and then pour over the meat. Place the lid on and cook for 4 hours on high or 8 hours on low.
3. Meanwhile, mix the parsley, lemon and garlic in a bowl and sprinkle it on top of the osso bucco before serving.

Nutritional Value (Amount per Serving):

Calories: 568; Fat: 38.09; Carb: 11.77; Protein: 43.16

Slow Cooker Lamb Shanks With White Beans

Prep Time: 15 Minutes
Cook Time: 4-8 Hours   Serves: 6

Ingredients:

- 3 tbsp olive oil
- 4 lamb shanks
- 2 medium red onions, chopped
- 2 cloves garlic chopped
- 2tbsp flour
- 1tbsp tomato concentrate
- 125ml balsamic vinegar
- 300ml red wine
- 150ml beef stock
- 1tsp fresh thyme, chopped
- 400g tin cannellini beans, drained and rinsed
- 2 medium carrots peeled and cut into 2cm dice
- 15g parsley, chopped

Directions:

1. Turn the slow cooker on so that its warm for the ingredients. In a large frying pan, heat 1 tbsp of the oil. Season the lamb shanks. Brown on all sides and remove.
2. Add the remaining oil and sauté the onion, garlic and some salt and pepper for 5 minutes. Add the flour and sauté for 2 mintues more. Add the tomato concentrate, vinegar, wine, stock and thyme, and bring to a boil. Pour into the slow cooker with the lamb, beans and carrots. Season once more and then place the lid over.
3. Cook on low heat for 8 hours or high heat for 4 hours. Do not lift the lid during cooking otherwise it will take longer. Skim any excess oil out with a large spoon. Serve with chopped parsley.

Nutritional Value (Amount per Serving):

Calories: 709; Fat: 12.02; Carb: 35; Protein: 24.22

Slow Cooker Lamb Rogan Josh

Prep Time: 2 Hours 30 Minutes
Cook Time: 6 Hours   Serves: 4

Ingredients:

- 700 g lamb neck fillet
- 1 large white onion sliced
- 2 tbsp oil
- or The Paste
- 3 tbsp tomato paste
- 3 garlic cloves minced
- 1½ tsp cumin
- 1½ tsp garam masala
- 1 tsp ground ginger
- ½ tsp ground black pepper
- 2 tsp paprika
- 1 tsp smoked paprika
- 1 tsp chilli powder hot
- 1 tsp salt
- 250 g natural yogurt not greek style set
- 1 red chilli finely chopped, seeds removed
- 1 tbsp cardamom pods pressed
- 1 tbsp chopped coriander dried or fresh
- 1 lamb stock cube crumbled
- 1 tbsp olive oil
- or The Sauce
- 400 g tomato passata
- 50 ml water
- 1 cinnamon stick
- 2 bay leaves
- 1/2 tsp sugar

Directions:

1. In a large bowl, mix together the ingredients for the paste until smooth.
2. Prepare the lamb fillet by removing any sinew and cutting into 3 - 4cm (1 - 1.5 inch) chunks. Add the lamb to the paste and stir to coat thoroughly. Leave for a minimum of 30 minutes, but ideally 2 hours (or overnight if preparing the night before).
3. Sear the marinted meat in a pan, along with the onions. Transfer to the slow cooker.
4. In another bowl, mix together the yogurt, coriander, sugar and chopped chilli and then gradually stir in the passata and water. This will ensure a smooth consistency.
5. Pour the sauce over the lamb and onions in the slow cooker, then add the bay, cardamon pods and cinnamon stick and ensure they are submerged in the sauce. Cook on low for 6 hours or high for 3.5 hours.

Nutritional Value (Amount per Serving):

Calories: 918; Fat: 52.69; Carb: 23.37; Protein: 87.74

Healthy Slow Cooker Apricot Lamb

Prep Time: 20 Minutes
Cook Time: 4 Hours 20 Minutes
Serves: 4

Ingredients:

- 2 tsp extra virgin olive oil
- 600g easy carve (boneless) lamb leg roast, excess fat trimmed, cut into 3cm pieces
- 1 large brown onion, cut into thin wedges
- 2 celery sticks, finely chopped
- 3 large carrots, peeled, sliced
- 2 tsp ground cumin
- 2 tsp ground coriander
- 1 cinnamon stick
- 500ml gluten-free Massel Salt Reduced Stock Chicken Style
- 1 tbsp pomegranate molasses
- 1 tbsp no-added-salt tomato paste
- 400g can no-added-salt chickpeas, rinsed, drained
- 90g dried apricots
- Fresh mint leaves, to serve
- 1 tbsp gluten-free cornflour
- Pomegranate arils, to serve

Directions:

1. Heat half the oil in a large non-stick frying pan over medium-high heat. (Alternatively, use the Browning function on the slow cooker.) Add the lamb . Cook stirring, for 3 minutes or until browned. Transfer lamb to slow cooker.
2. Return pan to medium heat. Add the onion , celery , carrot and remaining oil. Cook, stirring, for 3-4 minutes or until softened. Add cumin , coriander and cinnamon . Cook, stirring, for 2 minutes or until aromatic. Transfer to the slow cooker. Add the stock , molasses and tomato paste . Stir until combined
3. Cover and cook on High for 3-4 hours (or Low for 6-7 hours) or until the lamb is very tender, adding the chickpeas and apricots in the last 30 minutes of cooking.
4. Combine the cornflour and 2 tbs water in a small bowl. Add the cornflour mixture to the slow cooker and stir until combined. Cover and cook for 20 minutes or until the sauce thickens slightly. Sprinkle with mint and pomegranate arils to serve.

Nutritional Value (Amount per Serving):

Calories: 1016; Fat: 33.72; Carb: 137.99; Protein: 44.24

Slow Cooker Dhaba Lamb Curry

Prep Time: 20 Minutes
Cook Time: 5 Hours 20 Minutes   Serves: 4

Ingredients:

- 2 tbsp ghee
- 4 (about 1.5kg) lamb shanks, excess fat trimmed
- 2 large brown onions, finely chopped
- 4 garlic cloves, crushed
- 4 sprigs fresh curry leaves (about 10 leaves per sprig), plus 2 sprigs, extra
- 1 tbsp garam masala
- 1 tbsp ground cumin
- 1 tbsp ground coriander
- 1 tbsp ground paprika
- 2 tsp fenugreek seeds
- 80g natural cashews, coarsely chopped
- Steamed rice to serve
- Sliced cucumber to serve
- ½ tsp chilli powder
- 2 tbsp tomato paste
- 4 vine ripened tomatoes, chopped
- 2 tsp vegetable oil
- Natural yoghurt to serve (optional)
- Mango chutney, to serve (optional)

Directions:

1. Heat half the ghee in a large frying pan over high heat. (Alternatively, use the Browning function on a slow cooker.) Cook the lamb , in batches if necessary, turning often, for 8 minutes or until browned. Transfer to the slow cooker.
2. Heat the remaining ghee in the pan over medium-high heat. Add onion . Cook, stirring, for 10 minutes or until well browned. Add garlic . Cook, stirring, for 1 minute or until aromatic. Add curry leaves , garam masala , cumin , ground coriander , paprika , fenugreek and chilli . Cook, stirring, for 1 minute or until aromatic. Add the tomato paste . Stir until well combined. Add 60ml water and three-quarters of chopped tomato . Bring to the boil. Transfer to slow cooker. Cover. Cook on High for 5 hours or until the lamb is tender.
3. Just before serving, heat the oil in a small frying pan. Add the cashews and cook, stirring, for 2 minutes or until lightly toasted. Add the extra curry leaves and cook, stirring, for 2 minutes or until crisp.
4. Remove the lamb from slow cooker. Mash tomato mixture in slow cooker to thicken. Add the remaining chopped tomato. Season and stir. Return the lamb to sauce. Scatter over cashew mixture. Serve with rice , cucumber , yoghurt and chutney , if using.

Nutritional Value (Amount per Serving):

Calories: 495; Fat: 26.56; Carb: 38.59; Protein: 34.14

Chapter 5: Pork

Slow Cooker Pot Roast

Prep Time: 5 Minutes
Cook Time: 8 Hours   Serves: 4

Ingredients:

- 1.36 kilograms chuck roast
- 1 1/2 tsp. garlic powder
- salt
- pepper
- 0.68 kilograms potatoes (cut into chunks, see notes)
- 340 grams carrots
- fresh herbs (optional)
- 7 sprigs fresh thyme (optional)
- 2 sprigs rosemary (optional)

Directions:

1. Season the chuck roast on both sides with salt, pepper and granulated garlic
2. Optional: add fresh herbs, if desired. Rosemary and thyme are my favorites.
3. Cook on low in a slow cooker for 8 hours, until fork tender.
4. See notes for options regarding potatoes and carrots.
5. Pull apart with two forks, and serve.

Nutritional Value (Amount per Serving):

Calories: 646; Fat: 14.81; Carb: 60.14; Protein: 71.99

Slow Cooker Thai Pork With Peanut Sauce

Prep Time: 10 Minutes
Cook Time: 7 Hours   Serves: 4

Ingredients:

- 907.18 g boneless pork loin
- 2 red peppers diced
- 144 g teriyaki sauce
- 2 tbsp rice vinegar
- 1 tsp red pepper flakes
- 3 cloves garlic
- 2-3 tbsp peanut butter

Directions:

1. Combine all ingredients in a crockpot, cook on low for 7-9 hours
2. Shred and serve with rice

Nutritional Value (Amount per Serving):

Calories: 379; Fat: 11.15; Carb: 11.95; Protein: 54.41

Slow Cooker Pork Casserole

Prep Time: 15 Minutes
Cook Time: 6 Hours - 8 Hours Serves: 4

Ingredients:

- 1 tbsp vegetable or rapeseed oil
- 4 pork shoulder steaks (about 750g), cut into large chunks
- 1 onion, chopped
- 1 leek, chopped
- 1 carrot, chopped
- bundle of woody herbs (bouquet garni) – we used 2 bay leaves, 3 sage leaves and 4 thyme sprigs, plus a few thyme leaves to serve
- 1 chicken stock cube
- 2 tsp Dijon mustard
- 1 tbsp cider vinegar
- 2 tsp cornflour
- 1 tbsp honey

Directions:

1. Heat your slow cooker. Drizzle the oil in a wide frying pan over a high heat. Season the pork, then add to the hot pan. Avoid overcrowding the meat – you may want to do this in batches. Cook until deep brown all over, then transfer to the slow cooker. Add the onion and leeks to the frying pan and cook for a few minutes, until they soften. Add a splash of water and scrape any tasty bits from the bottom, then tip everything into the slow cooker. Add the carrot, herbs, stock cube, mustard and vinegar, season, then add enough water to just cover the ingredients. Stir, then set your slow cooker on low for 6-8 hrs, or high for 5-6 hrs.
2. In a saucepan, mix the cornflour and honey with 1-2 tsp of liquid from the slow cooker, until you have a smooth paste. Add 100ml more liquid, bring to a simmer until thickened, then stir back into the casserole. Serve with mash or dumplings, scattered with thyme leaves.

Nutritional Value (Amount per Serving):

Calories: 583; Fat: 36.56; Carb: 13.51; Protein: 47.67

Slow Cooker Pork Loin

Prep Time: 30 Minutes
Cook Time: 5 Hours - 6 Hours   Serves: 4-6

Ingredients:

- 1½ tsp fennel seeds
- 3 sprigs fresh thyme
- 2 garlic cloves
- 2 tbsp rapeseed or olive oil
- 300g shallots
- about 1.8kg pork loin, skin removed and fat well-scored (cut from the thicker end of the joint)
- 1 small celeriac, peeled, quartered and cut into chunks
- 2 eating apples, such as braeburns or coxs, peeled, cored and cut into wedges
- 150ml white wine
- 250ml chicken or pork stock
- 1 tbsp honey
- 1 tbsp Dijon mustard

Directions:

1. Lightly crush the fennel seeds with the leaves from the thyme and the garlic in a pestle and mortar. Add 1 tbsp oil and plenty of salt and pepper, then bash to a rough paste. Rub all over the pork, then cover and chill for up to 24 hrs, if you have time (2 hrs if not).
2. Set your slow cooker to a low heat. Pour a kettleful of boiling water over the shallots, then set aside for 2 minutes until cool enough to handle – this will make them easier to peel. Cut off the root and remove the papery skins. Heat the remaining oil in a large casserole or frying pan large enough to fit the pork. Brown the shallots for a few minutes then tip into the slow cooker. Add the celeriac and apples, season well and give them a mix.
3. Brown the pork in the same pan, on all sides, not forgetting the ends. Sit on top of the veg and apples, fat-side up, nestling the joint in a little so you can fit the lid on. Pour the wine into the frying pan and bubble for a minute, scraping the bottom of the pan to pick up any tasty bits. Pour in the stock, honey and mustard, bubble for another min, then pour over the pork. Cover with a lid and cook on low for 5-6 hrs (depending on slow cooker size), turning the pork and stirring the veg halfway through cooking.
4. Remove the pork, wrap in foil and leave to rest for 10 minutes before carving to serve alongside the veg with roast potatoes and greens.

Nutritional Value (Amount per Serving):

Calories: 847; Fat: 43.24; Carb: 23.03; Protein: 107.7

Slow Cooker Pork Fillet With Apples

Prep Time: 15 Minutes
Cook Time: 4 Hours   Serves: 4

Ingredients:

- ½ tbsp rapeseed oil
- 500g pork fillet, sliced into medallions
- 1 medium onion , finely chopped
- 3 eating apples
- 150ml low-salt chicken stock
- 1 tbsp Dijon mustard
- 4 sage leaves , finely sliced
- 2 tbsp half-fat crème fraîche

Directions:

1. Heat the slow cooker. Heat the oil in a large frying pan, fry the pork medallions on each side for 2 minutes until they pick up a little colour. Fry the onion for a few minutes, then add the stock and mustard to the pan and stir. Tip the pork and sauce into the slow cooker.
2. Core and cut the apples into quarters, add them to the pot with the sage. Season with black pepper. Cook on Low for 4 hours or until the meat is tender, then stir in the crème fraîche.

Nutritional Value (Amount per Serving):

Calories: 632; Fat: 34.1; Carb: 46.39; Protein: 35.32

Slow Cooker Pork Belly

Prep Time: 10 Minutes
Cook Time: 4 Hours And 20 Minutes
   Serves: 6

Ingredients:

- 3 garlic cloves, crushed
- thumb-sized piece root ginger, finely grated
- 3 tsp flaky sea salt
- 1 tbsp soy sauce
- 1 - 1.2kg pork belly, cut into 3 long strips, rind trimmed but fat left on
- 2 onions, sliced

Directions:

1. Mix together the garlic, ginger, salt and soy sauce then rub the mixture all over the pork belly. Put the sliced onion into the bottom of your slow cooker and place the pork belly pieces on top. Cook on high for 4 hours.
2. Carefully take the pieces of pork belly out of the slow cooker then transfer them to a non-stick frying pan with a good spoonful of the cooking juices, turning occasionally. Let sizzle away on a high heat until all the sides are browned and the liquid has evaporated. Slice or cut into wedges and serve with mashed potato, steamed green vegetables and a gravy made with the cooking juices. Alternatively use in a ramen noodle broth, bao buns or in your own recipe.

Nutritional Value (Amount per Serving):

Calories: 411; Fat: 27.73; Carb: 4.28; Protein: 34.01

Slow Cooker Goan Pulled Pork

Prep Time: 15 Minutes
Cook Time: 8 Hours And 10 Minutes
Serves: 6

Ingredients:

- 2 tbsp olive oil
- 1 large onion , halved and sliced
- 1 garlic bulb , cloves peeled
- thumb-sized piece ginger , shredded into very thin matchsticks
- 1 tbsp ground cumin
- 2 tbsp smoked paprika
- 2 tbsp ground coriander
- ½-1 tsp cayenne pepper (depending on how hot you like it)
- 225ml cider vinegar
- 2kg boneless pork leg or shoulder
- or The Salad
- 3 carrots , shredded with a julienne peeler or coarsely grated
- 1 red onion , finely chopped
- 3 tomatoes , chopped
- generous handful fresh coriander
- 1 lemon , juiced
- 1 tbsp olive oil
- 0 Serve
- 12 warm chapatis or small wraps

- chunky cucumber raita (see goes well with) and mango chutney

Directions:

1. Heat the oil in a large frying pan. Fry the onion, garlic and ginger for about 10 minutes. Stir in the spices, pour in the vinegar and stir well. Tip into the slow cooker (we used a 6.5-litre model) and add 1 tsp salt and about 20 turns of a black pepper mill. Add the pork joint, turn in the mixture to coat it, then arrange it in the pot so it is rind-side down. Cover and cook on low for 7-8 hrs.
2. Meanwhile, make the salad. Mix the carrot with the onion, tomato and coriander, then toss just before serving with the lemon juice and oil.
3. Remove the rind and fat from the pork and skim all the fat from the juices, then shred the meat into the juices. To serve, put some meat and salad on one side of a chapati, then top with the raita and chutney, fold over and eat with your hands.

Nutritional Value (Amount per Serving):

Calories: 562; Fat: 19.24; Carb: 18.7; Protein: 75.1

Chapter 6: Vegetable

Moroccan-Style Stuffed Peppers

Prep Time: 10 Minutes
Cook Time: 40 Minutes   Serves: 4

Ingredients:

- 2 large or 4 small red peppers, halved
- 150g couscous
- 300ml vegetable stock, just-boiled
- 400g tin chickpeas, drained and rinsed
- 100g feta, crumbled, plus extra to serve
- 100g semi-dried tomatoes, roughly chopped
- 50g green olives, chopped
- ½ lemon, juiced
- 3 tbsp olive oil
- coriander, chopped to make 2 tbsp, plus extra to serve
- 1 tbsp rose harissa

Directions:

1. Put the couscous in a heatproof bowl and pour over the stock. Cover the bowl and leave to stand for 5 minutes. Use a fork to fluff up the couscous, then stir through the chickpeas, feta, tomatoes, olives, lemon juice, olive oil, coriander and harissa. Season.
2. Fill the halved peppers with the couscous mixture. Put them into your slow cooker and put the lid on, then cook on the low setting for 6 hours. Then serve with the extra feta and coriander.

Nutritional Value (Amount per Serving):

Calories: 1078; Fat: 96.71; Carb: 50.18; Protein: 16.28

Slow Cooker Pearl Barley Risotto With Blue Cheese

Prep Time: 35 Minutes
Cook Time: 1 Hours 40 Minutes
    Serves: 6

Ingredients:

- 2 tbsp olive oil
- 50g butter, plus a little extra
- 3 large echalion shallots, finely chopped

- 3 celery sticks, finely diced
- 4 large garlic cloves, finely chopped
- 300g dried pearl barley
- ½ medium butternut squash (about 500g), peeled and deseeded, cut into 1.5cm cubes
- 75g Italian-style vegetarian hard cheese, finely grated
- 2 tbsp double cream
- 150g vegetarian blue cheese, crumbled, to serve
- or The Hazelnut Topping (Optional)
- 25g blanched hazelnuts, roughly chopped
- 2 tbsp olive oil
- 40g panko breadcrumbs (or leftover ciabatta crumbs)
- 1 sprig of rosemary, leaves only, chopped
- 25g Italian-style vegetarian hard cheese, finely grated
- zest of 1 lemon
- 200ml white wine or Prosecco
- 1.2 litres hot vegetable stock
- 1 bay leaf
- 2 sprigs of rosemary

Directions:

1. Preheat the slow cooker to low. Heat half each of the oil and butter in a large deep frying pan, add the shallots and celery and cook over a low heat for 10 minutes until softened. Stir in the garlic and cook for a further minute. Increase the heat and add the pearl barley, stirring for 1 minute.
2. Pour in the white wine, bubble for 2 minutes or until almost fully reduced. Transfer to the slow cooker, along with the hot stock, bay leaf and rosemary sprigs. Stir well; season. Cover with the lid and cook on the low setting for 1 hour.
3. Meanwhile, return the frying pan to a medium heat; add the remaining oil and butter. When hot, add the squash and increase the heat to high. Cook for 6-8 minutes, turning occasionally until golden brown on all sides. Transfer to a plate lined with kitchen paper and set aside.
4. After 1 hour the pearl barley should be almost tender. Stir in the squash and cook for a further 45 minutes-1 hour on the low setting until the stock has been almost fully absorbed, the barley is tender with a little bite, and the squash is cooked through. Switch off the slow cooker. Stir in the grated hard cheese and cream, season well and leave to sit for 5-10 minutes.
5. Meanwhile, make the topping: heat a large frying pan until hot, add the hazelnuts and cook over a low-medium heat until just toasted. Add the olive oil, breadcrumbs and rosemary and stir-fry over a low- medium heat until turning golden. Mix in the cheese and lemon zest; season and cook for 3-4 minutes, stirring occasionally until crisp and fragrant. Tip onto a plate to cool.
6. When the risotto is ready, spoon into bowls. Top with the blue cheese and a

sprinkling of the hazelnut topping.

Nutritional Value (Amount per Serving):

Calories: 514; Fat: 29.27; Carb: 52.16; Protein: 13.58

Slow Cooker Ratatouille

Prep Time: 10 Minutes
Cook Time: 3 Hours 30 Minutes
Serves: 2

Ingredients:

- 1 aubergine
- 1 red onion
- 1 red pepper
- 1 green pepper
- 4 button mushrooms
- 1 tbsp of tomato purée
- salt
- black pepper
- 4 tbsp of basil

Directions:

1. Prepare the vegetables and cut them all into a 1cm dice. Add to the slow cooker with the purée, salt and pepper
2. Mix well until the purée is evenly distributed and cook on high for 3 1/2 hours
3. When ready to serve, chop the basil and stir it through the ratatouille.

Nutritional Value (Amount per Serving):

Calories: 71; Fat: 0.4; Carb: 16.69; Protein: 2.72

Slow Cooker Onion Dip

Prep Time: 15 Minutes
Cook Time: 2 Hours   Serves: 4

Ingredients:

- 320 g Vidalia Onions chopped
- 216 g swiss cheese shredded
- 373.33 g mayonnaise
- 1/4 tsp garlic salt

Directions:

1. Spray crock pot with non-stick spray.
2. In a medium bowl combine onions, cheese, mayonnaise, and garlic salt.
3. Pour into crockpot.
4. Cover and cook on high for 2-3 hours stir once every hour.
5. Serve with baguette slices or wheat crackers.

Nutritional Value (Amount per Serving):

Calories: 532; Fat: 44.74; Carb: 11.86; Protein: 20.75

Slow Cooker Spinach Artichoke Dip With Sun-Dried Tomatoes

Prep Time: 10 Minutes
Cook Time: 1 Hour 30 Minutes
Serves: 12

Ingredients:

- 55 g sun-dried tomatoes chopped
- 150 g artichoke hearts diced
- 312 g chopped spinach frozen
- 115 g sour cream
- 112 g mozzarella shredded
- 1 garlic clove

Directions:

1. Combine sun-dried tomatoes, artichokes, and garlic in crockpot.
2. Cook on high for 35 minutes.
3. Add in sour cream, spinach, and mozzarella.
4. Cook on low for 45 minutes.

Nutritional Value (Amount per Serving):

Calories: 52; Fat: 1.32; Carb: 6.05; Protein: 5.31

Slow Cooker Ranch Carrots

Prep Time: 3 Minutes
Cook Time: 5 Hours   Serves: 6

Ingredients:

- 454 grams baby carrots (bag of)
- 2 Tbsp. ranch
- 473 ml vegetable broth

Directions:

1. Simply pour the bag of carrots in to your slow cooker.
2. Add the vegetable broth.
3. Stir in ranch seasoning.
4. Cook on high heat for 5 hours. At this point they should be just firm enough to hold their shape and not be too soft. Cook longer if you desire an even softer texture.
5. Serve warm or cool. Store extra carrots in the fridge.

Nutritional Value (Amount per Serving):

Calories: 727; Fat: 81.16; Carb: 6.52; Protein: 0.55

Slow Cooker Vegetable Stew With Cheddar Dumplings

Prep Time: 20 Minutes
Cook Time: 6 Hours   Serves: 6

Ingredients:

- 2 tbsp olive oil
- 200g baby carrots, scrubbed, trimmed and halved if large
- 3 leeks, cut into thick slices
- 3 garlic cloves, crushed
- 3 tbsp plain flour
- 400ml vegetable stock
- 2 courgettes, cut into large chunks
- 2 x 400g cans butter or cannellini beans, drained and rinsed
- 1 bay leaf
- 4 thyme, rosemary or tarragon sprigs
- 200ml crème fraîche
- 1 tbsp wholegrain mustard

- 200g broad beans or peas
- 200g spinach
- ½ small bunch of parsley, finely chopped, plus extra to serve
- or The Dumplings
- 100g self-raising flour
- 50g vegetarian suet or cold butter, grated
- 100g mature cheddar
- ½ small bunch of parsley, finely chopped

Directions:

1. Set the slow cooker to low. Heat 1 tbsp of the oil in a frying pan and fry the carrots for 5 minutes until just golden, then tip into the slow cooker.
2. Heat the remaining oil in the pan and fry the leeks with a pinch of salt for 5 minutes until soft. Add the garlic and stir in the flour. Gradually add the stock, stirring, until the flour has dissolved and there are no lumps. Bring to the boil, then tip into the slow cooker. Add the courgettes, beans and herbs, topping up with water to cover the veg, if needed. Cover and cook for 4 hrs.
3. To make the dumplings, tip the flour into a bowl and stir in the suet or butter until evenly distributed. Add the cheese, parsley, ½ tsp cracked black pepper and a pinch of salt. Mix in 3-4 tbsp cold water with your hands to make a soft, slightly sticky dough (add a little more water if needed). Divide into six and roll into balls.
4. Add the crème fraîche, mustard, broad beans or peas and spinach to the slow cooker and turn it to high. Arrange the dumplings over the stew, cover and cook for 1-2 hrs more until firm and doubled in size. Scatter with parsley and serve. Will keep for up to three days in the fridge or in the freezer for up to three months.

Nutritional Value (Amount per Serving):

Calories: 1298; Fat: 106.94; Carb: 52.85; Protein: 42.23

Chapter 7: Soups

Slow Cooker Chicken Soup

Prep Time: 15 Minutes
Cook Time: 6 Hours - 8 Hours   Serves: 6-8

Ingredients:

- 1 onion , finely chopped
- 2 celery sticks, finely chopped
- 2 carrots , chopped into 1.5cm pieces
- 2 leeks , halved and sliced
- 1 bay leaf and 3 thyme sprigs, tied together
- 1 whole medium chicken (about 1.4kg)
- 2l chicken stock
- 1 lemon , juiced
- ½ small bunch of dill or parsley, finely chopped
- crusty bread , to serve (optional)

Directions:

1. Set your slow cooker to low. Tip in the onion, celery, carrots and leeks and nestle in the bunch of herbs. Sit the chicken on top of the veg and pour over the stock. Cook for 6-8 hours.
2. Remove the chicken from the slow cooker and transfer to a board. Shred the meat from the bones using two forks, then return the meat to the slow cooker, discarding the bones. Season to taste and stir through the lemon juice.
3. Remove and discard the bunch of herbs. Ladle the soup into bowls and top with the dill or parsley. Serve with crusty bread, if you like.

Nutritional Value (Amount per Serving):

Calories: 401; Fat: 9.47; Carb: 15.37; Protein: 60.86

Easy Slow Cooker Butternut Squash Soup

Prep Time: 10 Minutes
Cook Time: 4 Hours 10 Minutes
Serves: 6

Ingredients:

- 1 large butternut squash, peeled and cut into large cubes
- 1 large onion, chopped
- 1 carrot, peeled and chopped
- 3 cloves garlic, crushed
- 4 sprigs thyme
- 1 sprig sage
- 720 ml low-sodium chicken (or vegetable) stock
- Salt
- Freshly ground black pepper
- Pinch of cayenne
- Double cream, for serving (optional)
- Freshly chopped parsley, for garnish

Directions:

1. In a large slow cooker, combine butternut squash, onion, carrot, garlic, thyme, and sage. Pour in stock and season with salt, pepper, and a pinch of cayenne.
2. Cover and cook until squash is very tender, on low for 8 hours or on high for 4 hours. Remove herb sprigs and use an immersion blender to blend soup until smooth.
3. Stir in cream and garnish with parsley before serving.

Nutritional Value (Amount per Serving):

Calories: 238; Fat: 12.33; Carb: 17.54; Protein: 17.45

Slow Cooker Chicken Noodle Soup

Prep Time: 10 Minutes
Cook Time: 6 Hours 30 Minutes
Serves: 6-8

Ingredients:

- 700 g boneless skinless chicken breasts
- 1 large onion, chopped
- 3 carrots, peeled and sliced into coins
- 2 stalks celery, sliced
- 4 tsp. sprigs fresh thyme
- 4 tsp. sprigs fresh rosemary
- 3 cloves garlic, crushed
- 1 bay leaf
- salt
- Freshly ground black pepper
- 2 l low-sodium chicken stock
- 250 g pappardelle

Directions:

1. In a slow cooker, combine chicken, onion, carrots, celery, thyme, rosemary, garlic, and bay leaf and season generously with salt and pepper. Pour in stock.
2. Cover and cook on low, 6 to 8 hours. Remove chicken from slow cooker and shred with two forks. Discard herbs and bay leaf. Return chicken to slow cooker and add pasta.
3. Cook on low, covered, until al dente, 20 to 30 minutes.

Nutritional Value (Amount per Serving):

Calories: 315; Fat: 12.06; Carb: 13.54; Protein: 35.85

Slow Cooker Beef Barley Soup

Prep Time: 20 Minutes
Cook Time: 8 Hours   Serves: 4

Ingredients:

- 700 g braising steak, cut into 5cm pieces
- Salt
- Freshly ground black pepper
- Extra-virgin olive oil, for drizzling
- 3 cloves garlic, crushed
- 1 onion, diced
- 2 carrots, cut into half moons
- 2 tsp. fresh thyme leaves
- 200 g mushrooms, cut into 1/2cm slices
- 50 g pearl barley
- 1 l chicken stock
- 1 tbsp. soy sauce

Directions:

1. In a large mixing bowl, pat beef dry with paper towels. Season generously with salt and pepper.
2. Preheat a large cast iron pan over high heat. Drizzle with olive oil and sear meat on all sides until golden brown with a crust, 8 to 10 minutes. Transfer meat to the slow cooker. Reduce heat to medium and add garlic, onions, carrots and thyme and season with salt and pepper. Scrape the pan with a wooden spoon to loosen all browned meat bits and cook 3 to 4 minutes. If needed, add a splash of water to fully deglaze the pan; transfer to slow cooker.
3. Add mushrooms, barley, stock and soy sauce; cook on low for 8 hours. Meat should be very tender.
4. Serve immediately.

Nutritional Value (Amount per Serving):

Calories: 1045; Fat: 36.92; Carb: 54.72; Protein: 126.3

Slow Cooker Carrot And Coriander Soup

Prep Time: 10 Minutes
Cook Time: 4 Hours 30 Minutes
Serves: 4

Ingredients:

- 700 g carrots
- 1 medium potato approx 100g
- 1 medium white onion approx 100g
- 1 garlic clove peeled
- 1 stock cube vegetable or chicken
- litre water
- 1 tbsp creme fraîche full or half fat
- 1½ tsp ground coriander
- ½ tsp turmeric
- ¼ tsp nutmeg
- 1 tsp butter
- ¾ tsp salt
- ⅛ tsp pepper pinch of ground black pepper

Directions:

1. Peel and chop the carrots into 1cm slices and peel and dice the potato in 2cm cubes. Peel and dice the onion. Put all the vegetables into the slow cooker with the clove of garlic.
2. Add the spices, stock, butter, salt and pepper to the vegetables.
3. Pour over the water and cook for 4½ hours on high or 6 hours on low.
4. Once cooked, transfer everything to a jug blender and blitz until the ingredients are roughly combined. Alternatively use a handheld blender and blitz in the slow cooker.
5. Add the creme fraîche and blend until completely smooth.
6. Finely chop the fresh coriander leaves and stalks and then sprinkle over the soup or stir them through before serving.

Nutritional Value (Amount per Serving):

Calories: 160; Fat: 1.58; Carb: 34.45; Protein: 3.92

Slow Cooker Tomato Soup

Prep Time: 10 Minutes
Cook Time: 4 Hours 15 Minutes
Serves: 4

Ingredients:

- 250 g Sweet Potato peeled and diced. This equates to roughly one baking sized potato. Use white potato as an alternative.
- 150 g carrots equates to two medium carrots, peeled and chopped.
- 2 400g canned tomatoes peeled plum tomatoes
- 1 white onion
- 4 tbsp tomato puree
- 2 vegetable stock cubes
- 1 tsp dried basil
- 1 tsp paprika
- ½ tsp garlic granules
- ½ tsp celery salt
- ½ tsp sugar
- 150 ml milk
- 250 ml water
- pinch of ground black pepper

Directions:

1. Peel and dice the vegetables into chunks of around 2cm or less. Add these to the slow cooker.
2. Add all of the remaining ingredients apart from the milk. Stir everything together.
3. Cook on high for 4 hours or low for 6 hours.
4. Check that the soup mixture is completely cooked through. The onions will be translucent and the vegetables can be easily sliced through with a knife. Then add the milk and cook for a further 15 minutes on high.
5. Next, carefully transfer the soup mixture to a jug blender and pulse until smooth. You can also do this with a stick blender directly in the slow cooker.
6. Serve immediately or allow to cool and store in the fridge or freezer.

Nutritional Value (Amount per Serving):

Calories: 368; Fat: 10.41; Carb: 69.54; Protein: 5.37

Chapter 8: Desserts

Slow Cooker Mac 'N' Cheese

Prep Time: 15 Minutes
Cook Time: 1 Hour And 30 Minutes
Serves: 4

Ingredients:

- 350g macaroni pasta
- 600ml whole milk
- 50g butter, cubed
- 50g soft cheese
- 100g mature cheddar, grated, plus extra to serve
- 20g parmesan or vegetarian alternative, plus extra to serve

Directions:

1. Pour boiling water over the pasta and drain, then put everything in a slow cooker and stir well. Season, cover and cook on low for 1 hr. Stir again, put the lid back on and cook for another 30 minutes until the pasta is cooked and the sauce has reduced enough to coat the macaroni.
2. Leave the lid off and reduce for the last 10 minutes if you need to, or add a splash more milk – this will depend on the size of your slow cooker and the brand. Serve with extra cheese.

Nutritional Value (Amount per Serving):

Calories: 528; Fat: 19.34; Carb: 71.58; Protein: 18.24

Slow Cooker Shepherds Pie

Prep Time: 1 Hour
Cook Time: 5 Hours   Serves: 4

Ingredients:

- 1 tbsp olive oil
- 1 onion, finely chopped
- 3-4 thyme sprigs
- 2 carrots, finely diced
- 250g lean (10%) mince lamb or beef
- 1 tbsp plain flour
- 1 tbsp tomato purée
- 400g can lentils, or white beans

Slow Cooker Cookbook for Beginners UK

- 1 tsp Worcestershire sauce
- or The Topping
- 650g potatoes, peeled and cut into chunks
- 250g sweet potatoes, peeled and cut into chunks
- 2 tbsp half-fat crème fraîche

Directions:

1. Heat the slow cooker if necessary. Heat the oil in a large frying pan. Tip the onions and thyme sprigs and fry for 2-3 minutes. Then add the carrots and fry together, stirring occasionally until the vegetables start to brown. Stir in the mince and fry for 1-2 minutes until no longer pink. Stir in the flour then cook for another 1-2 minutes. Stir in the tomato purée and lentils and season with pepper and the Worcestershire sauce, adding a splash of water if you think the mixture is too dry. Scrape everything into the slow cooker.
2. Meanwhile cook both lots of potatoes in simmering water for 12-13 minutes or until they are cooked through. Drain well and then mash with the crème fraîche. Spoon this on top of the mince mixture and cook on Low for 5 hours - the mixture should be bubbling at the sides when it is ready. Crisp up the potato topping under the grill if you like.

Nutritional Value (Amount per Serving):

Calories: 409; Fat: 8.22; Carb: 64.64; Protein: 27.77

Slow Cooker Fudge

Prep Time: 10 Minutes
Cook Time: 1 Hour Plus 4 Hours
Serves: 1

Ingredients:

- 375g can condensed milk
- 250g milk chocolate, chopped
- 250g dark chocolate, chopped
- 100g light brown soft sugar
- 1 tsp vanilla extract
- vegetable oil, for the tin

Directions:

1. Set the slow cooker to low (we used a 6-litre cooker). Tip in the condensed milk, both chocolates, the sugar, vanilla and a pinch of salt. Cook for 1 hr, stirring well with a spatula every 15 minutes to combine and scrape off any bits that start to stick to the bowl, until thick and smooth. Oil a 20cm square tin, then line with baking parchment. Pour the fudge mixture into

the tin and chill for 4 hrs.
2. Cut the fudge into 36 squares using a sharp knife. Will keep in an airtight container in the fridge for three days.

Nutritional Value (Amount per Serving):

Calories: 69; Fat: 3.95; Carb: 7.31; Protein: 1.11

Slow Cooker Muscovado Cheesecake With Hazelnuts Blackberries

Prep Time: 30 Minutes
Cook Time: 2 Hours   Serves: 10

Ingredients:

- 50g butter, melted, plus extra for greasing
- 225g oat biscuits (such as Hobnobs)
- 100g blanched hazelnuts
- 250g light muscovado sugar
- 4 tbsp full-fat milk
- 750g full-fat cream cheese
- 2 tbsp plain flour
- 1 tsp vanilla extract
- 3 large eggs
- 200ml pot soured cream
- 1 tbsp Frangelico (optional)
- 2 tsp cornflour
- 3 tbsp golden caster sugar
- 200g blackberries

Directions:

1. Boil the kettle and prepare your slow cooker (at least 22cm wide). Make a trivet for your cheesecake by scrunching a long piece of foil into a sausage. Roll into a loose coil and put on the bottom of the slow cooker. Turn the slow cooker to high and pour in enough hot water to come 4 cm up the sides. Wrap the outside of a 20cm springform cake tin in two layers of cling film and then foil – make sure there are no gaps for water to seep in. Grease the inside with butter, line with cling film and grease again, then line the base and sides with baking parchment.
2. Tip the biscuits and 50g hazelnuts into a food processor and blitz to fine crumbs. Add the butter and blend again until well combined. Tip the crumbs into the tin – use a spoon to press into the base. Chill for 10 minutes.
3. In a saucepan, heat the muscovado and milk until the sugar has dissolved. Set aside to cool. In a bowl, beat the cream cheese, flour, vanilla and eggs

until smooth. Stir in the soured cream, Frangelico (if using) and cooled sugar mixture until well combined. Pour into the tin and carefully put it in the slow cooker. Wrap the lid in a tea towel to prevent condensation from dripping onto the cheesecake. Cover and cook for 2 hrs, then turn off the slow cooker. Leave the cheesecake inside without opening for another 2 hrs. Remove from the slow cooker and cool at room temperature for a further 1 hr, then chill for 4 hrs, or overnight.

4. Put the cornflour, caster sugar and half the blackberries in a saucepan and set over a high heat. Cook for 3-4 minutes, squashing the blackberries a little, until syrupy. Toss in the remaining berries, heat through, then remove from the heat and cool until you're ready to serve. Roughly chop the remaining nuts and toast in a frying pan.

5. To serve, carefully remove the cheesecake from the tin, remove the baking parchment and transfer to a plate or cake stand. Top with the berries and hazelnuts, and serve with a shot of Frangelico, if you like.

Nutritional Value (Amount per Serving):

Calories: 405; Fat: 28.15; Carb: 28.15; Protein: 11.96

Slow Cooker Apple Crumble

Prep Time: 14 Minutes
Cook Time: 3 Hours 30 Minutes
    Serves: 4

Ingredients:

- 5 Granny Smith apples, peeled, cored and each cut into 8 wedges
- 1 tsp ground cinnamon
- 1 orange, zested and half juiced
- 60g rolled oats
- 50g walnut pieces
- ½ tsp ground ginger
- 75g plain flour
- 85g light muscovado sugar
- 90g unsalted butter, melted

Directions:

1. Put the slices of apple in a slow cooker. Sprinkle over the ground cinnamon, orange zest and 1 tbsp juice and mix together.
2. Put the oats and walnuts into a food processor and pulse a few times to give the texture of very course breadcrumbs. Pour into a bowl.
3. Stir the ginger, flour and sugar into the oat and walnut mixture then add

the butter and mix well.

4. Spoon the crumble mix over the apples, covering them all. Lay two sheets of kitchen paper or kitchen roll on top of the crumble. Cover with the slow cooker lid and cook on a low heat for 3½ hrs.
5. Remove the kitchen paper and cook for the last 10 minutes with the lid just slightly ajar.

Nutritional Value (Amount per Serving):

Calories: 462; Fat: 23.79; Carb: 60.42; Protein: 9.03

Slow Cooker Triple Chocolate Chip Cookie

Prep Time: 10 Minutes
Cook Time: 2 Hours 30 Minutes
Serves: 8

Ingredients:

- 100 g dark chocolate, broken into pieces
- 100 g butter, softened
- 100 g light brown soft sugar
- 75 g caster sugar
- 170 g plain flour
- 30 g cocoa powder (about 2tbsp)
- 1 large egg
- 1 tsp. vanilla extra
- 1 tsp. baking powder
- 100 g white chocolate chips
- 100 g mini Reece's pieces
- Vanilla ice cream and toffee sauce, to serve

Directions:

1. Grease bowl of your slow cooker with butter. Using two strips of parchment paper, line the bowl in an "x" formation. This will stop the cookie from sticking to the bottom.
2. In a bain marie, melt the chocolate, then leave to cool slightly. Using an electric mixer, beat butter and sugars until light and fluffy, about 2 minutes. Slowly beat in egg, vanilla extract and melted chocolate.
3. Add flour, cocoa powder, baking powder, and salt and stir until fully combined. Fold in chocolate chips and Reece's pieces. Pour cookie dough into slow cooker and smooth top with a spatula.
4. Cover and cook on high for 2 1/2 to 3 hours (or low for 5 to 6 hours), or until the cookie is almost completely cooked through and only slightly soft in the centre.

5. Cut into wedges and serve with toffee sauce and vanilla ice –cream.

Nutritional Value (Amount per Serving):

Calories: 490; Fat: 24.11; Carb: 64.43; Protein: 6.96

Slow Cooker Cinnamon Rolls

Prep Time: 20 Minutes
Cook Time: 2 Hours 25 Minutes
Serves: 8

Ingredients:

- or Cinnamon Rolls:
- Cooking spray
- Plain flour, for surface
- 400 g ready rolled pizza dough
- 110 g packed brown sugar
- 1 tsp. cinnamon
- 1/4 tsp. ground nutmeg
- 4 tbsp. melted butter
- or Frosting:
- 115 g cream cheese, softened
- 125 g icing sugar
- 1 tsp. vanilla extract
- 1 tbsp. double cream

Directions:

1. Line the bowl of a slow cooker with parchment and grease with cooking spray. On a lightly floured surface, roll out dough.
2. In a medium bowl, combine brown sugar, cinnamon, and nutmeg. Brush dough all over with melted butter, then sprinkle with brown sugar mixture.
3. Starting with one end, roll dough up tightly into a log. Slice into 8 rolls, about 3cm. Place rolls into prepared slow cooker. Place a paper towel under lid and cook on high for 2 hours.
4. Use parchment to remove cinnamon rolls from slow cooker and let cool while making frosting.
5. In a large bowl, beat together cream cheese and icing sugar until no lumps remain. Add vanilla and double cream and beat until combined.
6. Frost cinnamon rolls and serve warm.

Nutritional Value (Amount per Serving):

Calories: 324; Fat: 13.06; Carb: 44.83; Protein: 6.83

CONCLUSION

Are slow cookers necessary? You might not, sadly. Both a simple dutch oven and slow cooker can help you dine on a budget. However, if your busy schedule prohibits you from being in the kitchen prior to mealtime, a slow cooker is the answer. Dinner can be prepared in a slow cooker and left to cook unattended until you arrive home.

APPENDIX RECIPE INDEX

C
Carrot Cake Porridge 20

E
Easy Slow Cooker Butternut Squash Soup 59

G
Guinness Corned Beef And Cabbage 34

H
Healthy Slow Cooker Apricot Lamb 41

M
Moroccan-Style Stuffed Peppers 51

S
Slow Cooker Bread Recipe 18
Slow Cooker Bread 19
Slow Cooker Stuffing Recipe 20
Slow Cooker Cherry Oatmeal 21
Slow Cooker Banana Oatmeal 21
Slow Cooker French Toast 22
Slow Cooker Sweet And Sour Chicken 24
Slow Cooker Chicken And Prawn Paella Recipe 25
Slow Cooker Chicken Tikka Masala 25
Slow Cooker Chicken Mushroom Pie Filling Recipe 26
Slow Cooker Cream Cheese Chicken 27
Slow Cooker Teriyaki Chicken 28
Slow-Cooker Sweet And Sour Chicken 29
Slow-Cooker Spiced Beef Brisket With Cranberries ... 31
Slow Cooker Chinese Beef Broccoli 32
Slow Cooker Crock Pot Tater Tot Casserole Recipe 34
Slow Cooker Brisket With Golden Ale Gravy Horseradish Mash 35
Slow Cooker Lamb Osso Bucco 38
Slow Cooker Lamb Shanks With White Beans .. 39
Slow Cooker Lamb Rogan Josh 40
Slow Cooker Dhaba Lamb Curry 42
Slow Cooker Pot Roast 44
Slow Cooker Thai Pork With Peanut Sauce 44
Slow Cooker Pork Casserole 45
Slow Cooker Pork Loin 46
Slow Cooker Pork Fillet With Apples 47
Slow Cooker Pork Belly 47
Slow Cooker Goan Pulled Pork 48
Slow Cooker Pearl Barley Risotto With Blue Cheese And Squash 51
Slow Cooker Ratatouille 53
Slow Cooker Onion Dip 53
Slow Cooker Spinach Artichoke Dip With Sun-Dried Tomatoes 54
Slow Cooker Ranch Carrots 55
Slow Cooker Vegetable Stew With Cheddar Dumplings 55
Slow Cooker Chicken Soup 58
Slow Cooker Chicken Noodle Soup 60
Slow Cooker Beef Barley Soup 61
Slow Cooker Carrot And Coriander Soup 62
Slow Cooker Tomato Soup 63
Slow Cooker Mac 'N' Cheese 65
Slow Cooker Shepherds Pie 65
Slow Cooker Fudge 66
Slow Cooker Muscovado Cheesecake With Hazelnuts Blackberries 67
Slow Cooker Apple Crumble 68
Slow Cooker Triple Chocolate Chip Cookie 69
Slow Cooker Cinnamon Rolls 70

W
Winter Slow Cooker Beef Braise With Redcurrant Port Sauce 33

Printed in Great Britain
by Amazon